Looking Closely

around the Pond

FRANK SERAFINI

Kids Can Press

Look very closely.

What do you see?

Seashells?
Butterfly wings?
What could it be?

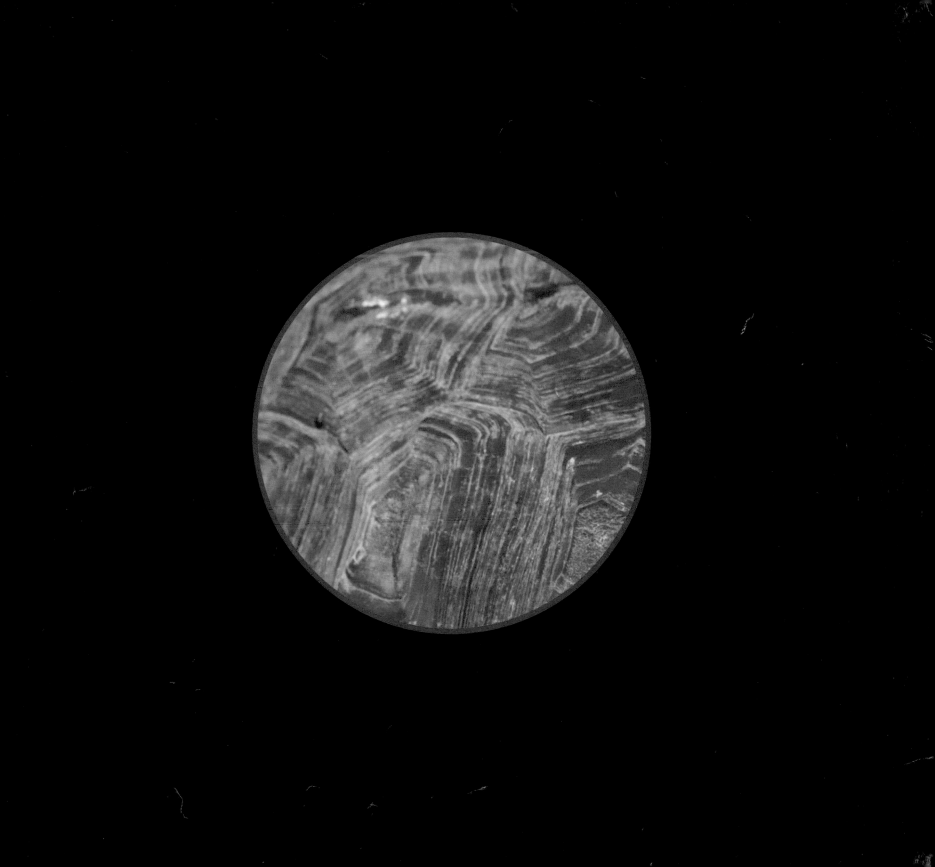

It's a Box Turtle.

Box turtles are shy creatures. They creep slowly around the pond, eating snails, mushrooms and small berries. They stay close to shore because they are not very good swimmers. In winter, box turtles dig into the ground. There, they sleep, or hibernate, until spring.

The colorful designs on a box turtle's shell help it to blend in with grasses. When a box turtle gets scared, it pulls its legs and head inside its shell to protect itself.

Look very closely.

What do you see?

Mars?
Jupiter?
What could it be?

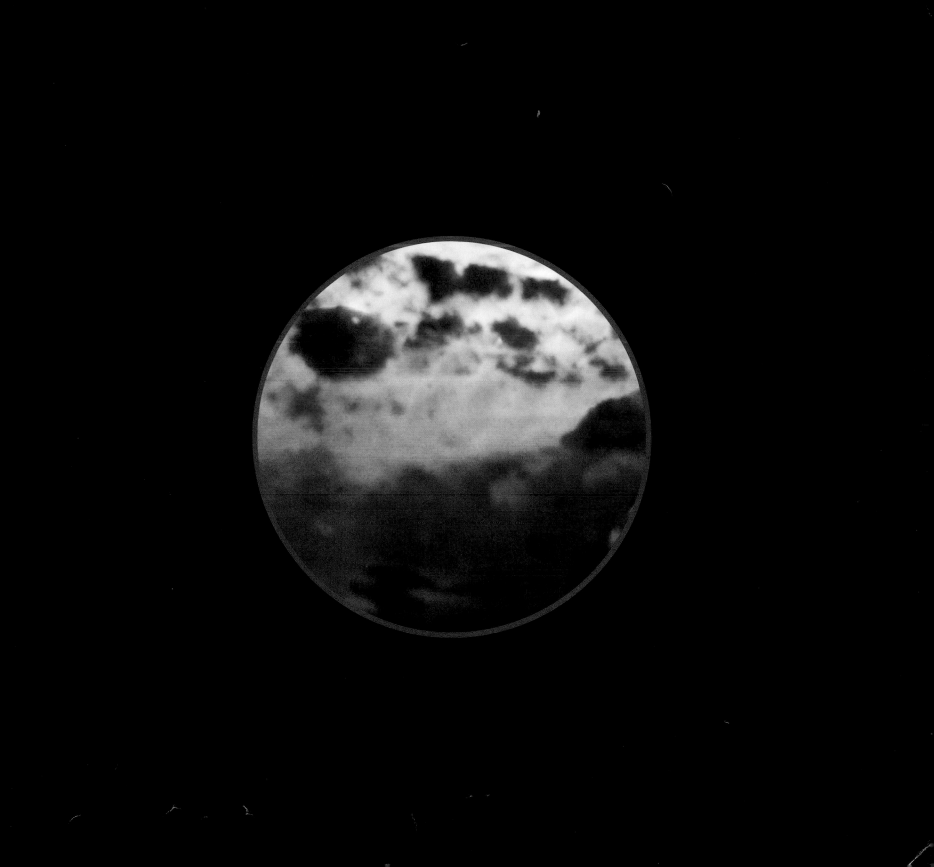

It's a
Shubunkin.

Shubunkins are members of the goldfish family. They originally came from Asia. Now they decorate people's ponds around the world. Shubunkins like to live with other fish in groups, called schools. They eat both plants and small insects and can grow to about 15 cm (6 in.) long.

Because shubunkins have three or more colors, they are sometimes called calico goldfish. The color blue is the rarest among these beautiful, strong swimmers.

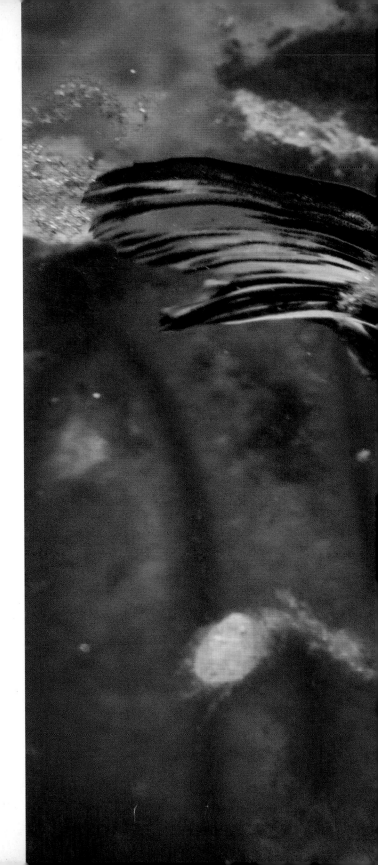

Look very closely.

What do you see?

Swirls of paint?
A snowy day?
What could it be?

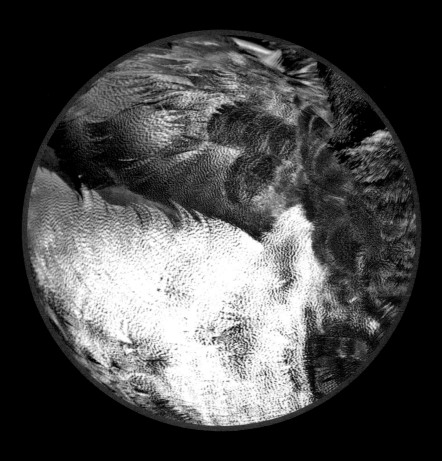

It's a Mallard Duck.

The mallard duck is easy to spot. As with most birds, the male, or drake, is more colorful than the female, or hen. Drake mallards sport emerald green feathers on their heads. Hens have brown feathers that blend in with their environment.

Mallard ducks are dabbling ducks. This means that they dip their heads underwater to find food. They eat seeds, plants and insects. In spring, mallards build their nests along the banks of the pond. The nests are often hidden inside a bunch of tall grass or cattails.

Look very closely.

What do you see?

A leaf?
A net?
What could it be?

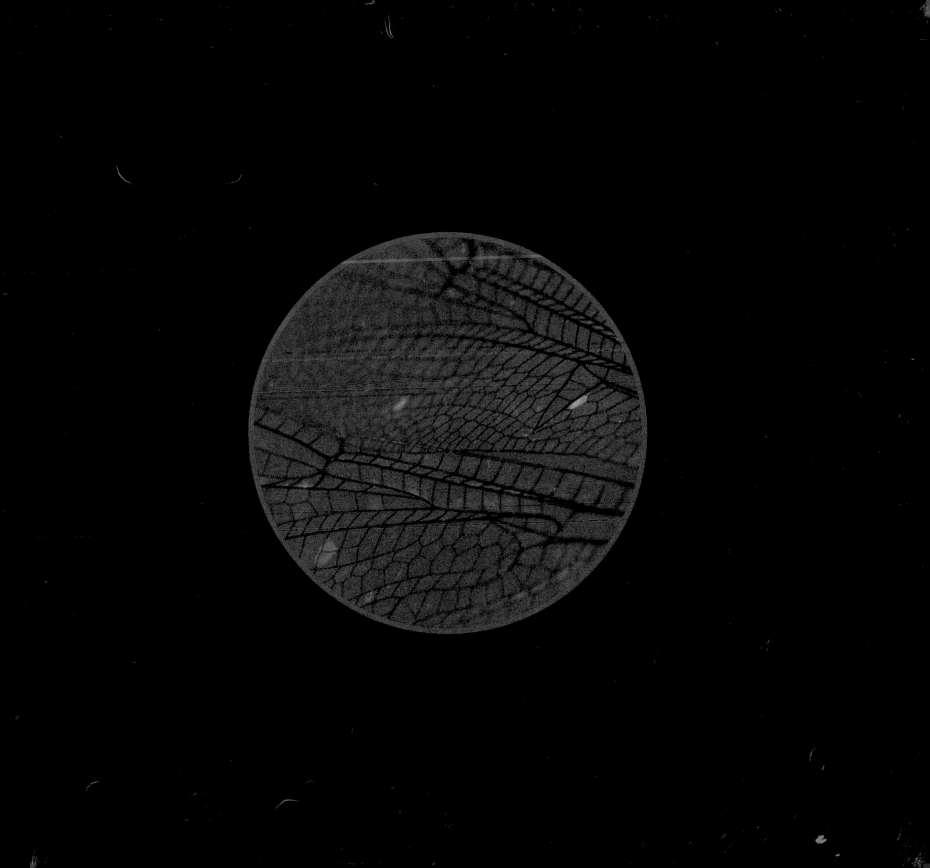

It's a Dragonfly.

For millions of years, dragonflies have roamed Earth. They were around even before the dinosaurs! Dragonflies begin their lives underwater as nymphs. When a nymph is almost fully grown, it climbs out of the water. Its skin splits open, and an adult dragonfly emerges with four transparent wings, like a butterfly from a cocoon.

In summer, you will find dragonflies skimming along the surface of the pond, darting back and forth, searching for food. Dragonflies have very large eyes and powerful jaws. They use these to snatch flies and mosquitoes right out of the air!

Look very closely.

What do you see?

Worms?
Matchsticks?
What could it be?

It's a Water Lily.

Water lilies float on the surface of the pond. Their waxy flowers are surrounded by large, round leaves. Water lilies bloom in many different colors, such as pink, white and yellow. These sweet-smelling flowers open up in the morning and close at night.

The stalk of the water lily reaches down to the bottom of the pond like an anchor. Fish, salamanders and frogs hide among water lily stalks. The plant's leaves and roots are food for beavers, deer and even moose.

Look very closely.

What do you see?

A night sky?
An autumn leaf?
What could it be?

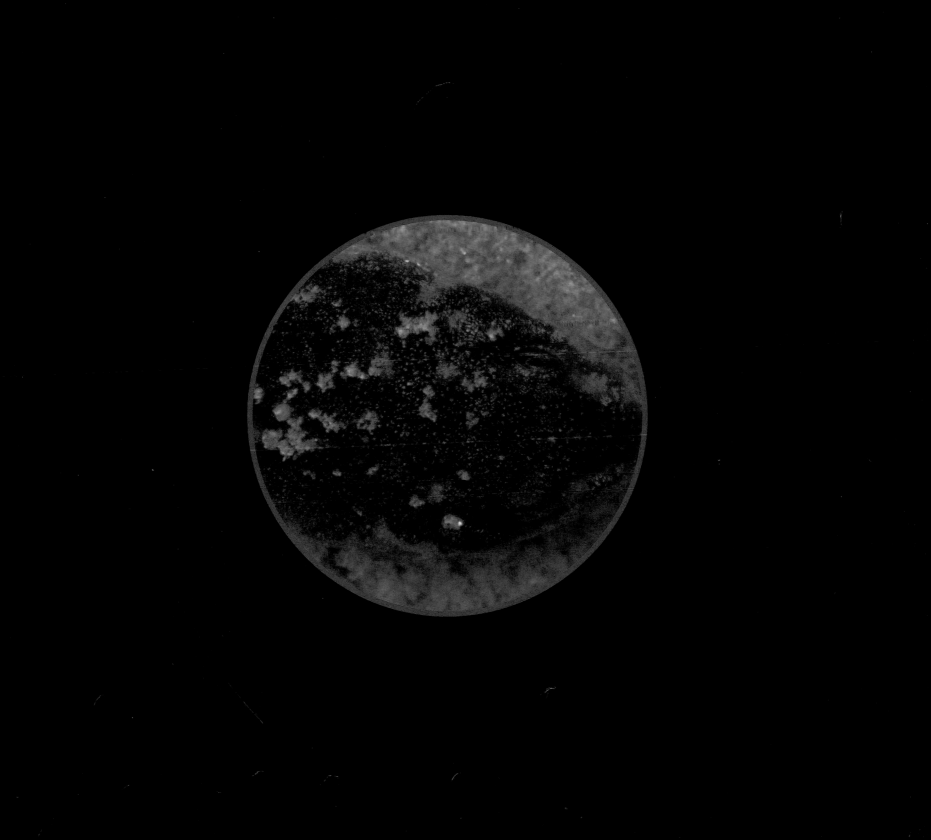

It's a Tadpole.

Frogs, toads and salamanders begin their lives as tadpoles. These animals are amphibians, which means they spend time in the water and on land. When tadpoles live in the water, they have gills. Like fish, they can breathe underwater. They eat algae and underwater plants.

As tadpoles grow older, their gills turn into lungs so that they can breathe above water. They grow legs, and they crawl out of the pond to live on land.

Look very closely.

What do you see?

A hot dog?
A chocolate bar?
What could it be?

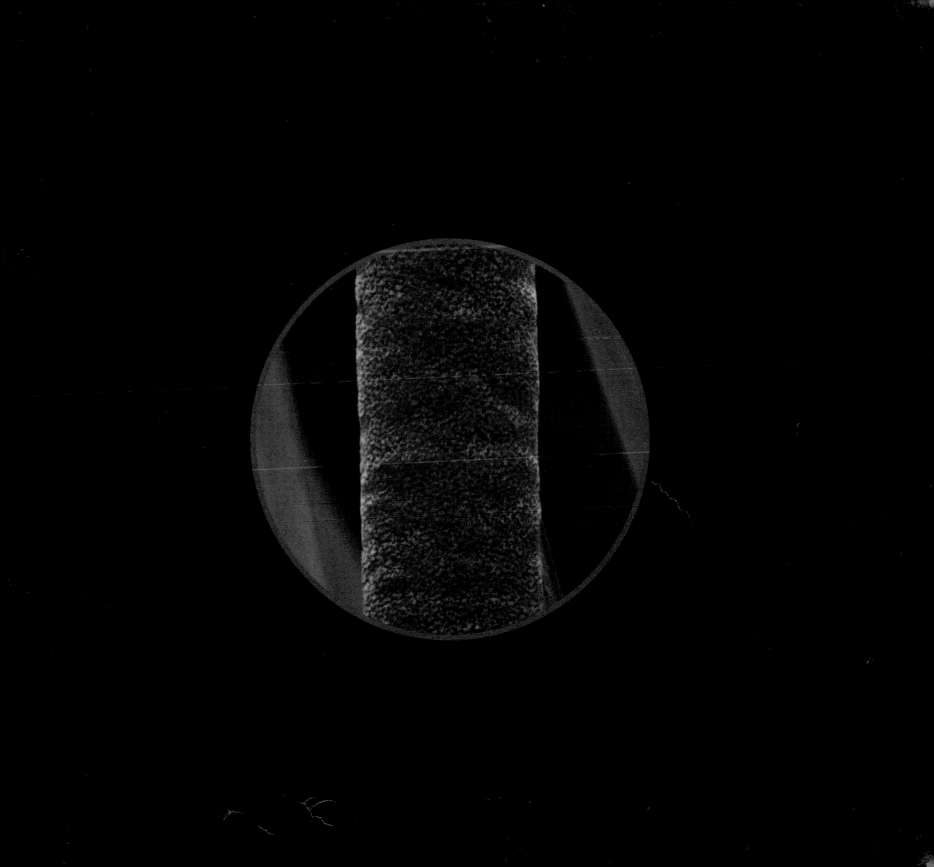

It's a Common Cattail.

Cattails grow in groups along the edges of the pond. They can reach up to 3 m (10 ft.) high — that's tall enough to hide a moose!

These plants are called cattails because their long, velvety seed heads look like cats' tails. Birds pick the fluffy seeds and use them to line their nests. Ducks build their nests among cattail stems. The plants also make a good hiding place for fish, frogs and turtles.

Look very closely.

What do you see?

A black snake?
A river of ink?
What could it be?

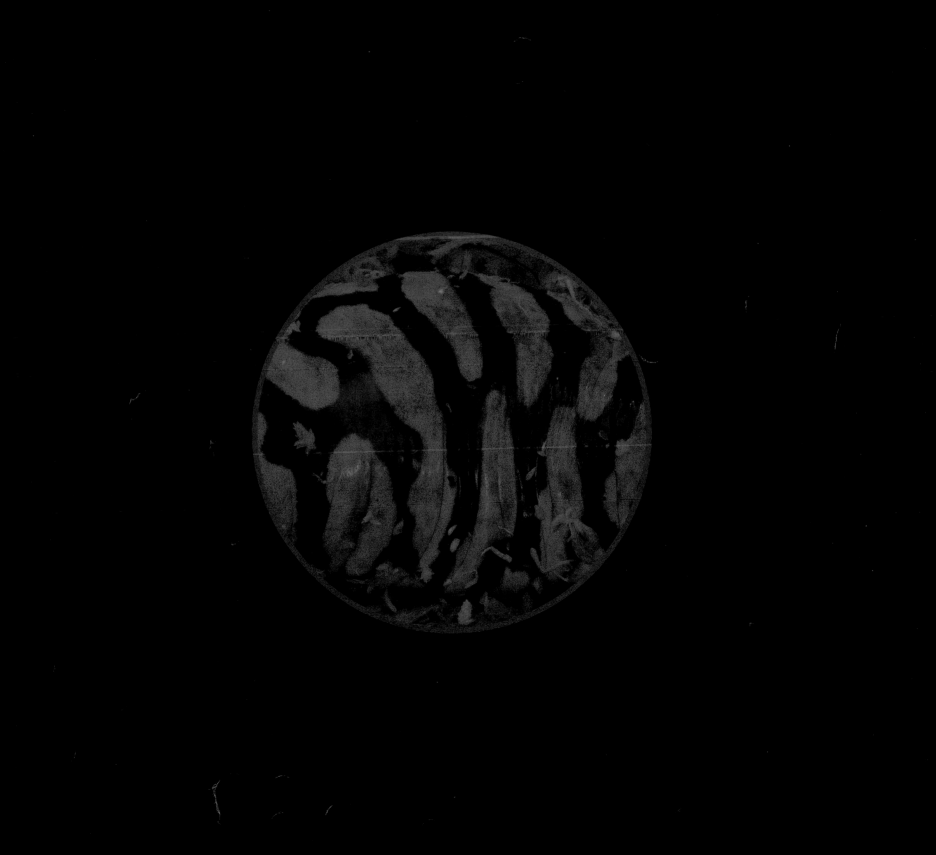

It's a
Tiger
Salamander.

Tiger salamanders start life as tadpoles. After they leave the pond, tiger salamanders dig and live in burrows, only coming out at night. They use their sticky tongues to catch insects and worms to eat.

Tiger salamanders hide in grasses around the pond. Their beautiful black and yellow stripes make them hard to spot. If you do find one of these creatures, don't touch it! The skin of the tiger salamander is easily hurt.

Look very closely.

What do you see?

A warty toad?
Broccoli?
What could it be?

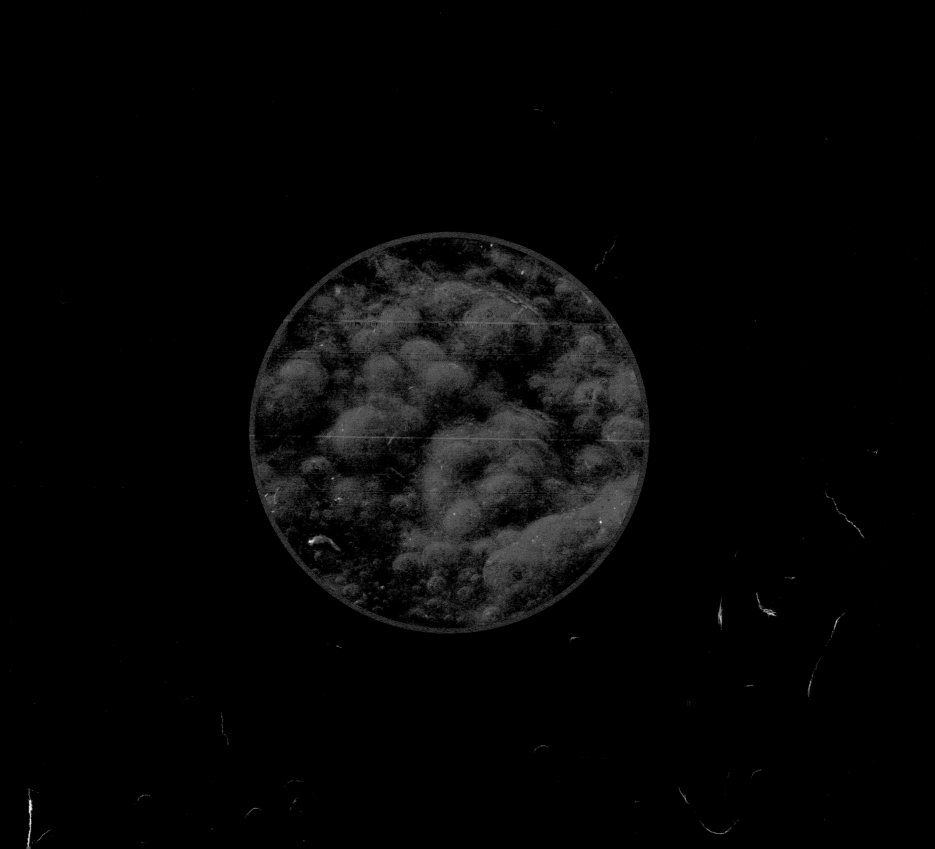

It's Green Algae.

Algae have grown on Earth for over 400 million years. Most plants that live in the water belong to the algae family. Some algae have funny names, like beard, fuzz and smear algae. Seaweed is a form of algae.

In ponds, most algae look like slimy green hairs. Many pond animals depend on algae for food. Ducks, fish, salamanders, snails and frogs all eat algae. Some kinds of algae make great plant food, too!

To Benjamin Chance Crippen, and his parents Cris and Kent.
Thanks for always letting me "pop in."

Photographer's Note

Photographers pay attention to things that most people overlook or take for granted. I can spend hours wandering outdoors in my favorite places looking for interesting things to photograph. My destination is not actually a place, but rather a new way of seeing.

It takes time to notice things. To be a photographer, you have to slow down and imagine in your "mind's eye" what the camera can capture. Ansel Adams said you could discover a whole life's worth of images in a six-square-foot patch of Earth. In order to do so, you have to look very closely.

By creating the images featured in this series of picture books, I hope to help people attend to nature, to things they might have normally passed by. I want people to pay attention to the world around them, to appreciate what nature has to offer, and to begin to protect the fragile environment in which we live.

Text and photographs © 2010 Frank Serafini

Pages 38–39: Lefferts Pond, USA Back cover: Willamette Valley, USA

Kids Can Press acknowledges the financial support of the Government of Ontario, through the Ontario Media Development Corporation's Ontario Book Initiative.

Published in Canada by
Kids Can Press Ltd.
29 Birch Avenue
Toronto, ON M4V 1E2

Published in the U.S. by
Kids Can Press Ltd.
2250 Military Road
Tonawanda, NY 14150

www.kidscanpress.com

Edited by Karen Li
Designed by Julia Naimska
Printed and bound in China

This book is smyth sewn casebound.

CM 10 0 9 8 7 6 5 4 3 2 1

Library and Archives Canada Cataloguing in Publication

Serafini, Frank
Looking closely around the pond / Frank Serafini.

(Looking closely)
ISBN 978-1-55337-395-7

1. Pond plants—Juvenile literature. 2. Pond animals—Juvenile literature.
3. Photography, Close-up. I. Title. II. Title: Around the pond. III. Series: Looking closely (Toronto, Ont.)

GB1803.8.S42 2009   j578.763'6   C2009-903623-1

Kids Can Press is a *corus*™ Entertainment company

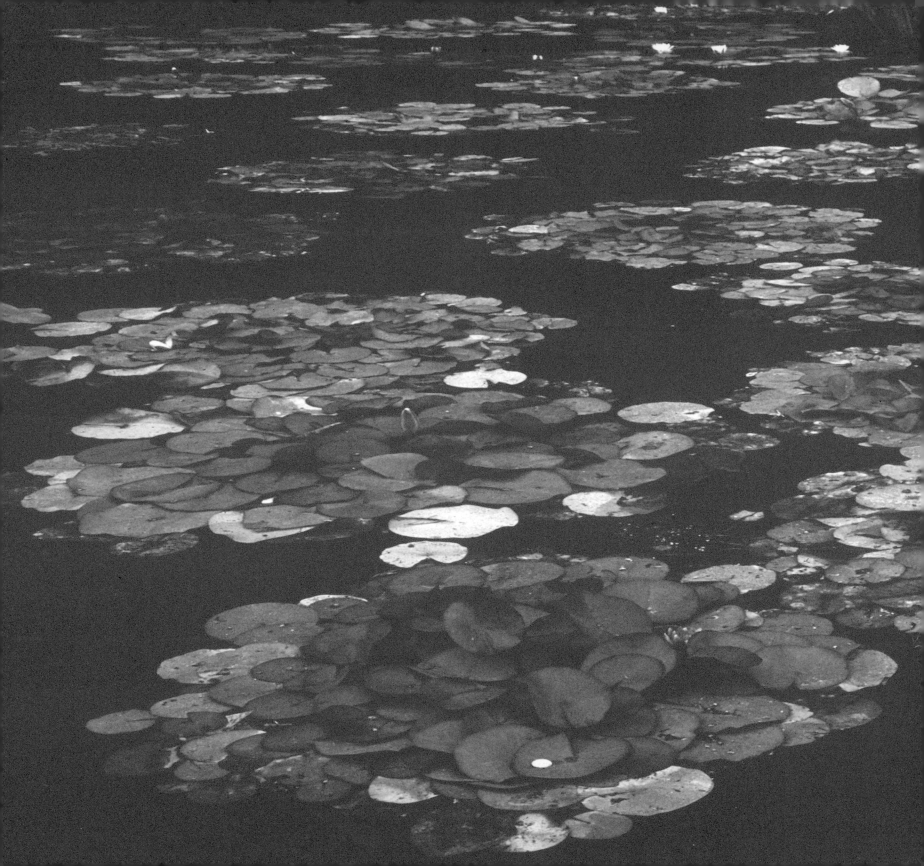